C000002196

Selected Poems

Gill McEvoy

First published 2024 by The Hedgehog Poetry Press

Published in the UK by
The Hedgehog Poetry Press
Coppack House, 5
Churchill Avenue
Clevedon
BS21 6QW

www.hedgehogpress.co.uk

ISBN: 978-1-916830-07-3

Copyright © Gill McEvoy 2024

The right of Gill McEvoy to be identified as the author of this work has been asserted in accordance with the Copyright, Designs and Patents Act 1988.

All rights reserved. No part of this publication may be reproduced, stored in or introduced into a retrieval system, or transmitted in any form, or by any means (electronic, mechanical, photocopying, recording or otherwise) without prior written permissions of the publisher. Any person who does any unauthorised act in relation to this publication may be liable for criminal prosecution and civil claims for damages,

9 8 7 6 5 4 3 2 1

A CIP Catalogue record for this book is available from the British Library.

Cover artwork © Gareth Morris

"He listens close with both his ears
and catches at the sound"

From "The Parrot" by William Cooper

For three remarkable people, Ciara, Treasa and Rory

Contents

Dairy-Room in the Old Farmhouse

Its silence pinions you
as if snakes had risen from its shelves
to turn you into stone.

Your skin goose-pimples
in the sweaty ooze from cold slate slabs.

Like an invisible fan
the seductive scent of cooling milk unfurls.

You scoop a thumb
through the slick of yellow cream,

wait till the hollow heals itself
and only then you swallow.

Catching the Turkey-Pluckers' Bus

7.30 a.m.
Tired workers with tired fingers,
thin stains of blood, feathers trapped
in the folds of their overalls.

The schoolgirls board the bus,
dust the seats off with their hands.

Later, in the breeze
from the one open classroom window,
feathers will float from a pocket,
from the crease of a pleat,
the elbow-crook of a blazer,

drift up in the air,
 so much chalk dust.

The Plucking Shed

As we pluck the air fills with a flour
of feather and dust. Everyone sneezes.
The floor is pillowed in down and quill.
Our footsteps smother in the folds of snow.

The plucking goes on and what you are
beneath your plumage shows itself:
enormous prickly pears, feather-pores
like craters in your skin.

On the floor your other selves,
the white plumed creatures
that we knew as geese,
grow light and tall.

Each time the door is opened
soundless skeins of ghosts rise up,
thread their way into the
blanket of the night.

Pig

Over her thirteen years of life
prolific litters squirmed against
her vast complacent sides.

He'd lean over the wall of her sty
for hours,
bring her offerings of cabbages,
corn stalks,
the incense, myrrh and gold
of beech nuts, acorns.

Shrouded in muslin,
glistening with salt
her earthly self was turned to
flanks of bacon, ham.

At mealtimes he'd hold her flavour
on his tongue,
stretch out a hand
as if to scratch once more her bristly back.

In the Butcher's Shop

Knives smack into flesh;
wet coats drip, rain plops
against the window glass

(blood falls drop by drop
in gutters in the abattoir).

Steam glistens on the sausage strings
hanging from the steel hooks.

The butcher's hands slap
bacon, pink as skin, on scales.
I look.

The smell of sawn bone
gravels in my throat.

Outside the rain's like new life on my face.
I'm running, running.

Puddles splash my ankles
with a kind of
grace.

Skinning Rabbits

You shot ten rabbits,
laid them on my doorstep with a note:
For your freezer, Merry Christmas!
They were like a problem
from my school-day maths I couldn't solve:
ten long leggy things
with soft grey fur and eyes like sad dead fish.
You had knotted their feet together
and when I lifted the bundle
they swung from my hands like heavy ropes.

I found my mother's pre-war cookbook.
It knew how to do those things that no-
one does:
cook in a haybox, pluck and dress a
fowl,
hang pheasants, make beef jelly.
Skin rabbits.
The steps exact. First, cut off the feet,
make an incision in the belly,
peel back the skin – like stripping a tangerine –
slip out the hind legs,
ease it over the buttocks,
up the spine, around the head,
down the front legs.
Discard.
Then gut and clean.

I didn't know that skin could look like that, that it
could hang so separate,
so sorrowful,
like single mittens children lose
and people place on railings.
The limp, moist bodies lay as innocent and pink
as babies after baths.
I could have hugged them up in big warm towels
and sung to them.

I knew I'd never eat them.

Preparing Fish

I have lived inland all my life,
got no further than sticklebacks
glowering in jars.

Here in my new kitchen
this strange fish slips from my grip,
slithers and slaps against the sink.
It smells of foreign things.

The loose scales must be scraped away:
I curse as, sliding, it escapes again.
But soon the sink begins to fill
with pieces of silver,

sequins sail its lake, starbursts
hammer its surface to shimmer.
 I scoop one gently on a fingertip;
it winks and winks with light.

When you walk in, starving as you say,
 you find me lining out frail specks
of starlight on the drainer's edge.

I Learn to Eat Fish with a Clear Conscience

because I have never fed a fish
from a bucket,
never put my milk-soaked fingers in its mouth
to teach it how to suck,
never stroked the head of a dying fish
I'd kept as pet,
never rugged a fish and walked it round the yard
till flesh and heart-rate cooled,
never watched a fish give birth,
nor seen a fish
leap fences in its urgency to find a mate,
never rubbed a fish's
rough-haired back.

Great-aunt Rose

Your great-aunt Rose, they'd start –
and you'd wriggle away with a book –
was a remarkable woman.
You flipped the page and went
on reading.

She had her own fleet of lorries
– what did lorries count for when you had
books and stories to explore?
And she transported fish, said dad.

From Grimsby. And she had her own name
painted on the lorries, added Grandad,
opening out his hands like a priest
distributing blessing.

You don't know where she took the fish,
you never asked. You do not know
who were the men who drove for her
or if she drove a lorry too?

Rose. Rose Archer. A name that makes
you think of her with bow and arrow
in her hand, shooting Pisces down from
nights as blue as sea.

For my Uncle

You were the one with an eye for the crowd:
in the grainy rain of celluloid,
the march of legs regular as pistons,
the greatcoats stiffly bonded row to row
we should have known it would be you

who lit the greyness with your startling smile,
broke the slope of guns to raise a cheerful hand,
saluting crowd and cameraman.

In the Garden I Search for You

(for my mother)

Silence.

Then, pale as the ghost swift moths
that dip and rise,
rise and dip
over the evening-primrose bed,

quick and small as the sparrow
searching the pea-pods,

insignificant mignonette
floods the air with sudden
scent.

Instantly you're there.

Sunday Lunch

She never gave up hope that he would want
the tender beef, the Yorkshire puddings
big as puffballs, the gravy rich with meat juice,
roast potatoes, lightly buttered beans and cabbage.
So she cooked all morning, from the very early hours, scouring the garden
for the firmest cabbage, sweetest beans, plundering the soil with her narrow
fork for white potatoes that came up on the new-turned earth like fresh-laid
eggs.

When we saw her worn boots leaning by the kitchen door
like two old horses barely up to standing,
we would know the scrubbing, chopping, sieving and salting had begun.
We heard the water running in the deep clay sink,
the chattering of knives, the wheel of the bean slicer crunching out green
slivers into china bowls.
We heard the raking of the black-range coals,
felt the kitchen growing large with heat.

If from his brick-built workshop we could hear the blue hiss of the solder
lamp, the hollow tap of hammers,
screech and scrape of metal, the low bass tump
of big-band radio, we knew that once again
he would not come in on time,
that he would curse her tender meat for tough,
the beans and cabbage underdone,
grumble that she piled his plate too high,
eat little, turn his nose up at the apple pie
and leave the table much too soon.

We understood the need to clean and grease all tools –
soap and lard in the kitchen, rags and oil in the shed.
Sunday nights we never understood
the restless creaking of their bed.

Lullaby for Grandma

Once the measured snick
of her mother's needles nudging
along the woollen rows
was a metronome for sleep.

Gone, along with wind-up clocks,
the hiss and plop
of gas and Tilley lamp,
the summer nightingale.

Now, in the long, long nights the old endure,
she lies there listening for the soothing
slip-tick-tack of someone knitting her
to sleep.

Scissors

Scissors, my mother told me when I was five,
was my first real world. That word, 'real', troubled me:
I had watched her hold her sheet of newsprint
over the mouth of the fire to make it draw,
seen how it singed in the middle, how the words
melted away, no longer real but gone.

The scissors remained, snipping, cutting,
slashing at things. *Dangerous. Don't touch.*
Always missing when she wanted them,
which made them somehow yet more real,
like a person whose absence is keenly felt.

The absence of you, for example, my father,
whose telephone number I still have by heart,
can still count on my fingers the things you kept
in your kitchen drawer: a knife, a fork,
one tablespoon, three teaspoons – the scissors,

that real word that had you, after my mother's death,
snicking at edges, severing frills,
shearing your life to so little.

Triple Rainbow

(for my father)

You had a driven need to simplify your life,
got down to one of everything, one chair, one bed,
one fork, knife, spoon.

When I came to visit you
I had to fill the car with everything you lacked,
a folding chair and bed, a mug, a plate and cutlery.

I'm driving from your funeral now;
torrential rain has plunged from clouds of black.

The sky is blue again, and in it,

parrot-brilliant,
a triple rainbow.

I hear you say,
I only needed one.

Losing Track

His file on the pin-wheel's pivot
sounds its careful scratch:
tick and scratch, scratch and tick
as the hands on each clock-dial
creep round. Or stick.

On the bench the baffling Arabic
of wheels, gut-lines, springs.
He fits his eye-glass firmly in, bends
to the demanding task of oil,
clean and mend.

Day shrivels into evening.
Outside, a blackbird's sudden squawk.

Its awkward chime reminds
the clock-restorer it is time.

Cellist

He opens the tall case, props it by the wall,
its twin halves like poppy sepals,
red silk showing inside.
He wheedles the cello into place,
spins it on its spiked heel like a top,
fits himself around it.

Like a long finger his bow comes searching,
choosing, over the strings.
And it begins:
dark river hum of sound,
and I

am driftwood swept away on water
and he is honey, oil, butter
oozing round the cello's curves.

The Bubble-Maker of Syntagma Square, Nafplion

He seats himself in the middle of the square,
surrounded by his bubble-launching gadgetry.
Children race to gather round him,
impatient for the count-down to begin.

Their parents, settled as the moons of Jupiter,
watch from pavement cafes.

Three, two, one! And lift-off! The bubble-man
lets fly great galaxies of teasing planets,
purpled moons and rainbow suns.

Eager to grasp a talisman of cosmos
the children soar into the night.
Leaping, laughing, running,
they bounce among a brilliance of stars –

small planets burst in their hands.

The Balloon Man

She stops to look at the man
twisting balloons into animal shapes.
She tugs her mother's arm.
What? snaps her mother whose mind's on shopping
and the fearful price of children's shoes.

Look mum, she says, *He's made a giraffe!*
and stands her ground as her mother tries
to drag her on.
The balloon man grins at her.
Not the honest grin of friendly adult
to enchanted child but a wolfish leer.

His spotted suit of purple, green and yellow
needs a wash
but the child only sees his fingers
flick as he fashions lions,
dogs and snakes and, yes – giraffe again!
She reaches out a hand,
touches its squeaky neck and laughs.

He leans down to stroke her cheek,
tickle her underneath her chin
when mother, noticing the man's duplicity,
 pulls the girl away. *Come on!*
she says.
But her daughter wails.
Hrrmph, her mother snorts, *did you
see the filthy state of his fingernails?*

Puddles

In the puddle water lies,
in the water stand the trees,
in the water there is sky,
reaching down, as she can see,
to where sky vanishes - but what
begins?

If she steps in she'll disappear,
go down and down
through clear, cold wet
till nothing will be left of her
(kitten in a sack plunged deep,
kitten only bubbles now).

Arms spread wide
like startled bird,
she teeters
on the puddle's edge,
her small heart rapid,
trembling -

Don't fall, don't fall,
don't ever let yourself fall in

The Padstow Hobby Horse.

It has no mane, no hooves; it prances and whirls
in front of her, a black cloth swirling round it.
She cannot see its eyes when it stops in front of her.

A choking neigh comes from its shapeless black,
like the awful sound that Terence made
the day their teacher led them past the open grave
of a class-mate who had died.

The walls of the grave were sweaty clay.
Water gleamed in a bottomless bottom,
white flowers were heaped beside it,
gathered ghosts of lost children.

Too much! She buries her head
between her grandad's knees and screams.
He pats her head, tells her it's alright.

But it's not alright.
The faceless thing is drumming its feet
in the road, whips up sand that stings her legs;
the air it parts is hot and stale,
and it's like no horse she's ever seen.

Grandad's Arm

When he explained about the arm
that hung so useless by his side
I only heard the word he used
and thought immediately of how it was
the sound of pebbles shovelled up the beach –
shrap, shrap, shrap –
the slap of waves as they collapsed
then the lulling sound as they withdrew –
nl-nl-nul.

I am ashamed to think now
of those metal splinters in his flesh,
the way he winced each time
I tried to hug him tight.

Visit from a Long-eared Bat

Fierce winds have flung you in from the night,
hurled you against the lit veranda wall,
a spatter of black mud. You cling.
We greet your strange arrival with delight.

We see the fishhook on your wing,
the thin vanes on its leathered fan
as you splay it out then draw it in,
your soft wax melting in and out of shape.

Your ears, black spathes of arum,
shiver to the echo of a moth in flight.

You've moved right round; now, upside-down,
could plummet any second

like a fat ripe plum,
splatter on the stones below,
stain them with the seep of sloe-dark blood.

The night is lashed by wind,
clouds claw across the moon's white face.

A moth blows in and batters at the lamp:
your sudden shadow shears my head.

The Bee-swarm

I dream we're running, stumbling over
the cattle-pocked ridges
of a dried-up marsh.

The wired air stacks current,
prickles rise on our arms.
Dark sky squats close to earth.

We reach the oak woods, sprint past
the great oaks, chestnuts, fast,
not to be trapped under trees in storm –

when you stop. And point. I pull you by the arm.
 No, you say, Look!

Alive as a broken ant-hill,
a huge melanoma heaving with cell division
hugs the shoulders of the oak.

Bees crawl, pour across each other,
wings loud in the crackling air.
I put my hand out, wanting to touch.
But my hand is stopped
by a sudden flash

as the first lightning zaps its neon
helter-skelter through the trees,
shocking the woods electric green.

Now it is you who pull me
by the arm. Hand in hand
we race through the woods
as the first great drops begin
to fall.

All the way I feel the strong
desire to look back.

Zoo

We had seen the tigers stretched out
in their jungle-garden, watched the condor
spread his wings to ease himself,

walked past zebra, camel, ostrich,
penguin and flamingo, all at anchor,
resting in the morning sun,

joined the milling crowd near the exit
when a flight of gulls went overhead,
their bellies dazzling in the light.

"Angels!" cried a little boy.
And everyone looked up.

Wilton Place, Dublin,1969

(for Derek Mahon)

Every bit the country gentleman back then.
Tweed jacket, twill trousers.

Shoes well polished.
Courteous manners.

And quiet, so quiet he never said
much about himself, only about poetry
or possibly a student.

We sat at break with our cups of tea
in a room dark with wood.

Had there been a green-shaded lamp,
a mahogany desk and a leather chair
it would have suited him well.

As would a pipe on which to
suck while he reflected.

Tea-break ended, his reflections
were never voiced.
He was probably always thinking

as he sat there with his cooling mug,
of that fungal shed in County Wexford,
the lost people of Treblinka.

The Ghost of Raftery the Blind Poet Visits Dublin

(Raftery, born 1779, blinded by smallpox when young,
became a wandering poet and fiddle player, creating
memorable songs and poems retained in popular memory.
Yeats' friend Lady Gregory first collected them)

The smack of footsteps like the bodhrán's drum,
the rattling shutters of the closing shops,
the slam of doors have drawn him here,
and, through the swooping, blinding rain,
 the traffic's swish and thrum.

Over these, a clear night-singer's song—
above an amber lamp a brave bird flutes
bright notes that pierce the sweep of rain.
Raftery joins the surge of ghosts that pour
unnoticed through the living throng,

marks the slow thud of the Gardai's tread,
the lively racket coming from the pubs,
drifts past the homeless scattered like the dead
(any one of these might be a second Raftery,
a wild fiddle tucked beneath his head.)

A taxi hisses past. He slips inside unseen,
eager to find the song that summons him:
 it's flung from the full throat of a thrush
that, unperturbed by stinging rain,
calls from a haloed crown of lime.

Two poets of eternal song for whom
the day and night are one, he plays his
unheard fiddle now for the bird that
sings on the glistening bough.

St Hwywyn's Church, Aberdaron

(the last parish church of the poet R.S.Thomas.)

What struck us was the sea-bright light of it,
the plain-wash white of it,
the damp and chill of it,
the sea-bird shrill of it,
the empty fill of it,

perched

on the egg-shell edge

between

a heaven of sky,
a hell of sea.

The Gravedigger

He leans his elbows on the straight-cut sides,
tells me he used a ladder when he first began –
Who would fancy being stuck down here? he grins,
Now, he says, he jumps – and shows me how,
touching his palms to the sore earth, springing out.

He's sun-baked like old pots,
says that's what he often finds down there -
fragments mostly.
He takes a flask of tea and offers me.
I shake my head. He lays his spade aside,
perches on a tombstone, motions me to do the same.
I refuse again.

He laughs. They'll never know, poor sods.
What matters is the living. The dead are solid weights
and it can be a nasty shock, that thud,
so me, I line my graves. Always.
Long grass is best,

especially after heavy rains –
no-one wants to hear that splash,
that can really set them off, s
o I line it good and thick,
the box will drop more gently then.

Later I think of all he said,
imagine lying for all eternity in the long grass,
almost envy the dead their luck.

Stepping into a Dress Made of Glass

(from an exhibition of glass corsets and dresses by Diana Dias-Leao)

These shaped petals of glass
would clutch your breasts tight,
their wires cut your skin,
burn you in the heat.

Think of the chatter and chink of ice
in winter, the wind's brass fingers
piercing the gaps.

But those pale roses
bordering its basque,
that fringe of silver reeds of glass —

for these you would step in,
and pull it tight, except

where once there were breasts
there are now rough scars
cross-hatching your chest

like the craquelure
in ancient glass.

Season of the Snowy Owl

*(There is a myth that an owl lays 2 eggs, one with power to
remove body hair, the other with power to restore it.)*

Months of living minus eyebrows, pubic hair,
or any hair at all – the ugly chick
that birds might root out from the nest.

You dropped the wrong egg in my hands,
struck the Arctic into me
with one white swoop.

Cat-owl, cat-face, cat-ogle —

(I saw cat in the man examining my body,
kneading my abdomen with his paws;
behind his glasses
feline yellow bloomed.)

I hid among rocks.

Winter came and you flew south
but first you laid in my hands
a second egg.

I nurtured it and when it hatched
I knew my body camouflaged in hair again.

Bearings

Fireflies fill the night with sparks –
flicker, flare, like faulty electricity.

She feels for the sandy track with naked feet.
The pines and hickories

have blocked out all the light.

In the dark the lake chill shocks her into gasp.

She wades waist-deep, stops
 to get her bearings.

In the round gap the trees have left,
so many stars the night can't breathe,

the water's mirror staggered by their weight.

She's swept round in a carousel of stars,
a dizzy spin of fireflies.

Salmon Run

Their rapid race towards the weir
flings them into air in arcs
of beaten silver light.

They leap and spring and play,
charging the afternoon with fire,
each fin a ridge of flame.

They reach the salmon ladder,
sinew up, go thrashing on.

And with them goes
the brilliance of the day,

leaving the river grey where briefly
it had danced and shone.

The Goosander

eats through the water's turmoil,
sharks round boulders,

folds his body in an arc,

dives below the fume of current
smoking over rocks.

At the snap of twigs beneath your feet

he spreads his wings,
snips the river clean in two,
is gone.

Glass Bird in a Shop Window

Surely the maker of this bird is one
whose winter months are lived
among deep silences of snow,

who understands the blue and purple
bruise of folds among the drifts,
who knows

the strange transparencies of ice,
the way light toes on it
a fragile dance?

I have been standing here so long
my feet have slipped into
fur-lined boots,

snow is settling on my shoulders
under dank green pine
and snow-locked birch.

Ice splits: a bird flies up,
freckles the freezing air
with blue.

A shudder of snow
ushers its escape.

Jade Plant

The earth is parched and shrinking,
the grass has given up its hold.

I think about water – we are all thinking about water –
there is a hosepipe ban in force and stringent warnings
to be frugal in our use of it.

I measure out mean cupfuls from the tap,
imagine (our bodies ninety percent water)
each cup as hand, foot, forearm.

On the windowsill above the sink
a jade plant, fat green money tree,
is flourishing,

every leaf a reservoir of hoarded wealth,

while *rain* now seems to me a word so beautiful
I roll it on my tongue like a wildly expensive taste,
chant it like a mantra,

rain, rain, rain, rain
as if in calling I could make it come.

Football, Kuala Lumpur

Rain loves this place, loves the way
the open hands of city trees receive it,
the way its great drops
trampoline the pavements.

It sends the people scattering for taxis,
forests of umbrellas sprung
like orchids opening.
It empties streets and

brings a thousand frogs
chuckling from the storm-drain walls,
calls out barefoot boys to football pitches
where they kick the ball

through floods of water,
spray and warm steam flying.
Arcs of rainbow fly from foot to foot,
shrieks of laughter mingle
with the chortling of frogs

that leap and spring
in their own games
on every pavement's edge.

Blakemere, Cheshire

The pines are muttering in tongues.
Beyond their black wall lies a shining lake,
loud with colonies of gulls.

I want to go there, search for
purple skullcap at the
water's edge.

Wind picks up, the trees
crack side to side like whips,
mutter turns to roar –

I run the terrifying
gauntlet of the pines
burst

into a First Created world,
silver with light and water,
glittering with wings.

Yellow Wagtail by the Canal

You bob beside the water,
feathered ball
of coltsfoot, celandine,

weave about the bank,
dipping, bowing,
wild daffodil in the wind.

A downy feather floats away,
bright pollen on the air.

Solving the Mystery of Darwin's Club-winged Manakin's Song

You baffled Darwin,
for even though your beak is closed you sing.
But now your secret's known:
you tip your body forward,
agitate your wings

and, like a plectrum thrumming
through the strings of a guitar or mandolin,
one wing feather's stiff bent tip
 skims down the adjacent quill whose shaft
is bare of vanes and ridged with ribs.

Exactly as the cricket plays its legs
along the saw-toothed edges
of its wings, you bow one perfect note on this,
your feathered violin.

Tiny bird with bright red head
you fling from your cunning feathering
your one exquisite note,
again, again, again.

Acknowledgements

Some of the poems are drawn from the following collections:

"Uncertain Days" (Happenstance Press, 2006); "The Plucking Shed", (Cinnamon Press, 2010); "Rise", (Cinnamon Press, 2013); "Are You Listening?" (Hedgehog Press, 2020)

My thanks to the editors of the following magazines/anthologies for the other poems:

Antiphon, Envoi, English: the Journal of the English Association, The North, The Rialto, The Michael Marks Award Anthology; Crannog, Stand, Agenda, Grey Hen Press, The Emma Press, Mslexia, Chester Academic Press, Dodging the Rain.